JOIN ME

16 JAZZ DUETS

for Two Clarinets

MUSIC MINUS ONE

Music Minus One

3250

CONTENTS

ISBN 1-59615-725-9

1. Togetherness

MMO 3250

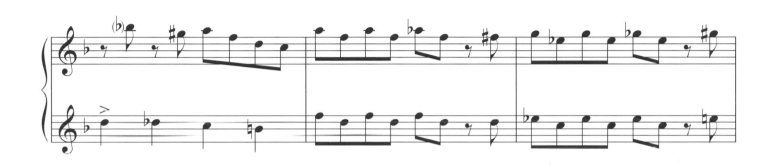

2. Jazzed Up Strauss

6 beats (2 measures) precede music.

Fast waltz ♩=168

3. A Swinging Big Band Sound For Two

Solo

4. Drawing Room Music With A Beat

6 beats (2 measures) precede music.

Fast waltz ♩=160

5. A Ballad With Release For Laughs

8 beats (2 measures) precede music.

Medium ♩=144

6. Dirty, Low Down Blues

7 beats (1 ¾ measure) precede music.

Slow blues ♩=76

7. More Big Band

8 beats (2 measures) precede music.

Medium fast ♩=160

8. Pretty Music

5 beats (1 ¼ measure) precede music.
(1 2 3 4 / 1)

Slow ballad ♩=72

18

9. Fun With Chord Progressions

8 beats (2 measures) precede music.

↓ 10 26

Medium bounce ♩=144

10. Very Fast, Light, Basie Touch

11. For Sheep Herders Only

4 beats (1 ¹/3 measure) precede music.

Slow waltz ♩=88

12. Jazz Chorus
With Light Background

7 beats (1 ¾ measure) precede music.

Medium bounce ♩=152

13. Not Recommended
For Arthritic Horn Players

9 beats (2 ¼ measures) precede music.

↓ **14** **30**

Very fast ♩=192

14. Chamber Music 1968

15. Music To Get Your Jollies By

8 beats (2 measures) precede music.

16. A Psychedelic Trip

JUST A SAMPLING OF ALBUMS FOR CLARINET FROM MUSIC MINUS ONE

Pop, Blues & Jazz Classics

Bluesaxe Blues for Saxophone, trumpet or clarinet — MMO CD 4205
Bob Johnson, tenor saxophone - Eric Kriss, piano & electric piano; Bob Johnson, tenor and soprano sax; Stan Poplin, acoustic and electric bass; Jim Chanteloup, drums: Eight original blues compositions covering a broad range of styles from boogie-woogie to gospel to modern funk, for piano, bass, drums and sax. Listen, then play along. Complete arrangements for both E-flat and B-flat instruments.

Tricky Dicky; When the Spirit; Cocaine Stomp; Wailer Blues; Boogie Breakdown; Tremblin'; Yacey's Fancy; Mad Dog Blues

Traditional Jazz Series The Condon Gang Adventures in New York & Chicago Jazz — MMO CD 3252
Bobby Gordon, clarinet - Hal Smith's Rhythmakers: Chris Tyle, trumpet; Clint Bakert, rombone; Anita Thomas, tenor saxophone; Ray Skjelbred, piano; Katie Cavera, guitar; Marty Eggers, bass; Hal Smith, drums: From the 1920s to the 1950s, Eddie Condon and his band created a unique style of traditional jazz, characterized by a succession of instrumental solos and abrupt transitions of dynamics; the result reverberates to this day in jazz. Now you can participate in this incredible style and the traditional music of the Condon Gang with this digital MMO release. A stellar lineup of professionals in a fabulous ensemble!

I Know that You Know; Strut Miss Lizzie; Jazz Me Blues; Skeleton Jangle; Monday Date; The One I Love Belongs to Somebody Else; A Kiss to Build a Dream on; I Must Have that Man; Georgia Grind

Days of Wine & Roses Sax Section Minus You — MMO CD 4210
Frank Wess, tenor sax - Bob Wilber All-Stars: Bob Wilber, soprano sax/clarinet; Hal McCusick, alto sax; Frank Wess, tenor sax/clarinet/flute; Joel Kaye, baritone sax & bass clarinet; Bernie Leighton, piano; George Duvivier, bass; Bill Goodwin, drums: Jazz legend Bob Wilber brings together a stylish set of classics scored for sax quartet, piano and rhythm section. The four-part voicing, a departure from the traditional big-band era five-man section, makes each voice all the more important and will enhance your pleasure in performing the missing part. Clarinetists will find all soprano parts easily playable; Tenor players can play the soprano parts directly with the added bonus of a chance to study the superb soloing of Frank Wess.

Moon Mist; Days of Wine and Roses; Acapulco Princess; Two Moods for Piano and Winds; The Mighty Hudson; Early Morning Blues

Easy Jazz Duets - Two Clarinets and Rhythm Section — MMO CD 3213
The Benny Goodman Rhythm Section: George Duvivier, bass; Bobby Donaldson, drums: A delightful collection of easy-to-medium duets featuring you plus an all-star fellow instrumentalist, clarinetist Kenny Davern and rhythm section. 1st to 4th year.

The Green Danube; Tone Colors; Reaching Up; Uptown-Downtown; Main Street; Ski Slope; Doing Your Chores; Stop and Go; Glider; Jumper; Da Dit; Hot Fudge; Tijuana; La De Da De; Switcheroo; Swing Easy; Hop Scotch; Swingin' in the Rain; 4/4 Waltz; One Note Break; Lazy; Bits and Pieces

For Saxes Only tenor sax, trumpet or clarinet — MMO CD 4204
Bob Wilber, tenor sax; Hilton Jefferson, alto sax - The Bob Wilber All-Stars: Bob Wilber, tenor sax; Hilton Jefferson, alto sax; Jerome Richardson, alto sax; Seldon Powell, tenor sax; Danny Bank, baritone sax; Dick Wellstood, piano; George Duvivier, bass; Panama Francis, drums: Designed to give the jazz saxophonist (or clarinet or trumpet player) an opportunity to play with a top-flight sax section. Due to the comparative scarcity of big bands today, this is the one area in which young players sorely lack experience. The problems of sight-reading, intonation, phrasing, vibrato, unisons, subtone, etc. which the player will encounter in working with this album are the same one would face playing with Ellington, Basie or Goodman. If you haven't had the opportunity to work in a big band, playing with this album should give you an idea of that special thrill one gets when the blend is perfect and everybody's swinging together!

Countdown; Might as Well Be Movin' On; Waltzing on a Reed; Ballad for Beth; Freemanition; Living for Love; Pork 'n' Beans; Blues for a Matador

From Dixie to Swing — MMO CD 3234
Kenny Davern, clarinet - Kenny Davern, clarinet & soprano sax; 'Doc' Cheatham, trumpet; Vic Dickenson, trombone; Dick Wellstood, piano; George Duvivier, bass; Gus JohnsonJr., drums: These Jazz legends back you up in this collection of 1950s 'Dixieland' standards performed in New York clubs such as Eddie Condon's and Nicks.. We encourage you as soloist to invent counter-melodies rather than mere harmony. This is a music of loose weaving parts, not one of precision ensemble figures. A great improvisational experience.

Way Down Yonder in New Orleans; Red Sails in the Sunset; Second Hand Rose; Rose of Washington Square; On the Sunny Side of the Street; Exactly Like You; I Want a Little Girl; The Royal Garden Blues

In a League of His Own *Pop Standards played by Ron Odrich and You* — MMO CD 3215
Ron Odrich, clarinet - The Al Raymond Orchestra; Mark Stallings, string synthesist: Join Ron in these pop classics. You won't be disappointed!

All or Nothing at All; Come Rain or Come Shine; Stardust; The Coffee Song; Days of Wine and Roses; Emily; I Hadn't Anyone 'Til You; I Concentrate on You; If I Should Lose You; It Might as Well Be Spring; Saturday Night (Is the Loneliest Night of the Week)

Isle of Orleans — MMO CD 3253
Tim Laughlin, clarinet - Tim Laughlin's New Orleans All-Stars: Native son Tim Laughlin decided he wanted to create in the style, but not necessarily using the tried and true classics, of the "Crescent City." So he assembled an extraordinary band of players, all veterans of the music, wrote a collection of new songs, and produced this extraordinary album. It won First Prize as the Best Jazz Album created in Louisiana in 2003 by Offbeat Magazine. Tim graciously made this album available to Music Minus One, remixing the music to omit the key players, clarinet, trumpet, trombone, piano, bass and drums for some of the most delectable play-alongs we offer in our catalogue. This is music rich in tradition but new to your ears. This music isn't easy but then again, to modern players, it may be, as they'll be able to negotiate the charts provided. We've provide audio samples of each song. This is music for the ages, guaranteed to pleasure players from ten to ninety. The personnel of this band is extraordinary as you can see, and the music they make together has to be experienced. Listen, can you hear that band? **(2CD Set)**

Magnolia Dance; Restless Heart; Blues for Faz; Suburban St. Parade; It's My Love Song to You; Gentilly Strut; I Know I'll See You Again; Crescent City Moon; Isle of Orleans; Monkey Hill

Jazz Standards with Rhythm Section — MMO CD 3218
Larry Linkin, clarinet - : Jazz standards with Larry Linkin as soloist guiding you. Then try them yourself with the rhythm section! **(2CD Set)**

Sweet Georgia Brown; Memories of You; Claire de Lune/Moon River; Oh, Lady Be Good; Porgy and Bess: *Summertime; Back Home Again in Indiana; Goodbye; One Note Samba; It Had To Be You; Autumn Leaves; Wolverine Blues; Amazing Grace; Here's that Rainy Day*

Jazz Standards with Strings — MMO CD 3219
Larry Linkin, clarinet - : Superb jazz standards with string accompaniments; work your own artistry with this great ensemble! **(2CD Set)**

When Sunny Gets Blue; What'll I Do; That's All; I've Got It Bad and That Ain't Good; In a Sentimental Mood; Our Love Is Here to Stay; Embraceable You; What Are You Doing the Rest of Your Life?; 'Tis Autumn; Night and Day; But Beautiful; Darn That Dream; Ain't Misbehavin'; When I Fall in Love

Lee Konitz Sax Duets — MMO CD 4110
Lee Konitz, saxophone - Lee Konitz and the MMO orchestra/various: Jam with the legendary Lee Konitz on this power-packed album of sax duets. Includes straight duets as well as duets with rhythm section and orchestral backgrounds! Features a wide range of music, from New Orleans to standards to Bossa Nova. Contains both E-flat and B-flat parts, and can be used by alto or tenor sax players, as well as clarinetists and trumpeters. You simply will not want to miss this album, one of the most requested classic titles from the vast MMO catalogue.

You Go to My Head; Meditation; Three Little Words; Somewhere; Blues in A-flat; Waltz; Free Form No. 1; Free Form Ballad; Basin Street Blues

Play Lead in a Sax Section — MMO CD 4209
Hal McKusick, solo alto saxophone - Bob Wilber All-Stars: Bob Wilber, soprano sax/clarinet; Frank Wess, tenor sax/clarinet/flute; Joel Kaye, baritone sax & bass clarinet; Bernie Leighton, piano; George Duvivier, bass; Bill Goodwin, drums: Sequel to 'For Saxes Only' offers a series of saxophone quartets (rather than the typical 5-piece arrangement from the big-band era). Hal McKusick provides a complete version to give samples for the improvisational sections, and you have the option of playing the notated solo, or improvising your own.

The Look of Love; All Too Soon; No More Blues; Century Plaza; In an Old Deserted Ballroom; A Little Farewell Music

Ron Odrich Plays Standards plus You — MMO CD 3220
Ron Odrich, clarinet - (rhythm section: A broad-based album of popular standards; listen to this master perform, then try it yourself with the rhythm section.

April in Paris; I Got Rhythm; Oh, Lady Be Good; Embraceable You; Porgy and Bess: *The Man I Love; Body and Soul; Poor Butterfly; What Is This Thing Called Love?; Lover Come Back to Me; I Only Have Eyes for You; Sometimes I'm Happy*

Sinatra Set to Music *Kern, Weill, Gershwin, Howard and You* — MMO CD 3216
Ron Odrich, clarinet - The Al Raymond Orchestra: Ron Odrich plays these great Sinatra standards, then you take center stage the second time around! Great pieces for improving your musicianship.

Steppin' Out with My Baby; That's All; Angel Eyes; It Was a Very Good Year; Embraceable You; Body and Soul; Fly Me to the Moon; Yesterdays; Prisoner of Love; Here's that Rainy Day; Speak Low

Southern Winds: Jazz Flute Jam — MMO CD 3376
Maurice Gainen, flute - The Maurice Gainen Band: Jazz master Maurice Gainen has assembled a stellar assortment of jazz standards with a quality all their own. Listen to Mr. Gainen's interpretations, then you join the ensemble as the star player! Includes C, B-flat and E-flat parts and is perfectly suited to virtually any instrument!

Little Linda; Black Orpheus; Blue Bossa; Meditation; Just Friends; Samba de Orfeo; Feel Like Makin' Love; Comin' Home Baby; Mercy, Mercy, Mercy

Stompin' & Struttin' the New Swing *Six Bands on a Hot Tin Roof* — MMO CD 3237
Around 1998, a new swing sound came to our music. Derived in part from the Big Bands of the Forties, and tempered by the music of such jump bands as Louis Prima and Louis Jordan, besides adopting the dress code of the hip-cats of an earlier era (Cab Calloway for instance) these bands played some great music in a more modern, flexible and fun-drenched style. We've taken the most famous songs of these groups, and put them all on an MMO CD for your pleasure and participation.

Hey, Pachuco; The Indigo Swing (style of Indigo Swing); Zip Gun Bop (style of The Royal Crown Review); Put a Lid on It (style of The Squirrel Nut Zippers); Hell (style of The Squirrel Nut Zippers); You and Me and the Bottle Makes Three Tonight (Baby) (style of Big Bad Voodoo Daddy); Zoot Suit Riot (style of The Royal Crown Review); The Ding Dong Daddy of the D-Car Line (style of The Cherry Poppin' Daddies); Jump, Jive & Wail (style of The Brian Setzer Orchestra); This Cat's on a Hot Tin Roof (style of The Brian Setzer Orchestra)

Traditional Jazz Series: Chicago-Style Jam Session — MMO CD 3239
Evan Christopher, clarinet - Jon-Erik Kellso, trumpet; Mike Pittsley, trombone; Brian Ogilvie, tenor saxophone; Jeff Barnhart, piano; Bill Huntington, guitar; Jim Singleton, bass; Hal Smith, drums: This exciting 2-CD set emphasizes collectively improvised ensembles and the succession of individual solos in the freewheeling "Chicago-Style" offshoot of New Orleans Jazz. The rhythmic texture is rooted in the swing feel of the late 1930s, and the instrumentation is typical of the New York groups of this genre. The songs are popular melodies from the 1900s to 1930s as well as multithematic compositions and blues—you'll find such classics as "'Deed I Do," "Sugar," "The Darktown Strutters' Ball," "That's a Plenty" and more. Chicago-style jazz is named for the city where it first developed. In the 1920s, many New Orleans musicians, including "Jelly Roll" Morton, Louis Armstrong, the Original Dixieland Jazz Band, and the New Orleans Rhythm Kings actively performed and recorded in Chicago. Many younger musicians were profoundly influenced by their music, including Eddie Condon, Benny Goodman, Gene Krupa, Muggsy Spanier and many others. By the 1930s many of these same musicians moved on to New York. As the Big Band era closed, improvising soloists still found work in New York clubs such as Nick's, Condon's and the Metropole. The texture was distinctly in the New Orleans tradition but the language was Swing and directly reflected the synthesis that took place in Chicago. This stylistically accurate recording demonstrates the inner workings of collective improvisation in a traditional jazz context. You'll be blown away by the quality of this jazz combo. Includes both printed solo part and a concert lead sheet, to give you a rare glimpse into the workings of the bands of the times. **(2CD Set)**

The Darktown Strutters' Ball; That's A Plenty; Rosetta; Poor Butterfly; Sugar (That Sugar Baby o'Mine); 'Deed I Do; Blues (My Naughty Sweetie Gives to Me); The Royal Garden Blues

Visions The Clarinet Artistry of Ron Odrich — MMO CD 3214

Ron Odrich, clarinet - Lew Soloff, trumpet/flugelhorn; David Fink, bass; David Ratajczak, drums; John Basili, guitar Sammy Figueroa, percussion; Marc Copeland, piano; John Corbert, synthesizer/Larry Fallon (Arranger): Match skills with one of the finest clarinetists in jazz with original material and standards, ballads and Latin stylings, plus an exquisite classical selection. Both the listening and the playing are exceedingly exciting and worthwhile. For intermediate-to-advanced players. Enjoy! **(2CD Set)**

I Love You Just the Way You Are; Two for the Road; El Cajon; Concerto in C minor: *II. Adagio; Only Trust Your Heart; Daphne's Vision; Highway Vision; Visions of Nina Marie; A Vision of the Hamptons; It Might as Well Be Spring; Street of Dreams; My Foolish Heart*

When Jazz Was Young — MMO CD 3829

Bob Wilber All Stars: Bob Wilber, clarinet; Buck Clayton, trumpet; Vic Dickenson, trombone; Bud Freeman, tenor sax; Dick Wellstood, piano; Abdul Malik, bass; Panama Francis, drums: One look at the player's list on this album will reveal some of the most famous veterans of the jazz era ('30s through '60s). An opportunity to jam with these jazz giants should not be missed. Under the leadership of Bob Wilber (he scored the film 'Cotton Club'), they present a memorable hour of music-making you'll not soon forget!

Keepin' out of Mischief Now; Chimes Blues; High Society; A Star Is Born: *The Man that Got Away; Do You Know What it Means to Miss New Orleans; Tin Roof Blues; Wild Man Blues; Milenberg Joys; Wolverine Blues; When the Saints Go Marchin' in (arr. Bob Wilber); Basin Street Blues*

Student Series

Baermann Method, op. 63 The Virtuoso Clarinetist — MMO CD 3240

John Cipolla, clarinet - piano accompaniment: A landmark recording of the entire Carl Baermann Method for Clarinet, the original and still most authoritative clarinet study. This first volume contains the complete opus 63 plus extensive notes on performance. Produced by John Cipolla, teacher, soloist and recitalist. A primary tool for teaching the clarinet—a master class! **(4CD Set)**

Baermann Method, op. 64 The Art of the Clarinet — MMO CD 3241

John Cipolla, clarinet - keyboard accompaniment: The second half of MMO's classic recording of the entire Carl Baermann Method for Clarinet, the most revered and complete clarinet 'method' ever produced. Contains the complete opus 64 and extensive performance notes. Produced by John Cipolla, teacher, soloist and recitalist. **(4CD Set)**

Classic Themes *Student Editions, 27 Easy Songs - 2nd-4th year* — MMO CD 3245

Harriet Wingreen, piano: Familiar world classics for clarinet and piano. Perfect for the intermediate player.

Albéniz *Tango;* Cohan Little Johnny Jones: *The Yankee Doodle Boy;* Curtis *Come Back to Sorrento;* Donato *A Media Luz;* Dvorak *Humoresque No. 7, op. 101, no. 7; Slavonic Dance;* Foster *Beautiful Dreamer;* Händel Xerxes (Serse), HWV40: *Largo;* Ivanovici *Waves of the Danube;* Key *The Star Spangled Banner;* Lehár *Gold and Silver (waltz);* Lemare *Andantino;* Leybach *Fifth Nocturne;* Offenbach *Apache Dance;* Les Contes d'Hoffmann (Tales of Hoffman): *Barcarolle (Moderato);* Pestalozza. *Ciribiribin;* Rubinstein *Melody in F, op. 3, no. 1;* Schubert *Moment Musical;* Ellens Gesang III: *'Ave Maria', op. 52, no. 6;* J. Strauss, Jr. *Blue Danube (waltz), Tales from the Vienna Woods;* Tchaikovsky *None but the Lonely Heart (Nur wer die Sehnsucht kennt), op. 6, no. 6;* Trad. (English folk song) *Country Gardens (English folk song);* Trad. (Gypsy melody) *Two Guitars;* Trad. (Gypsy song) *Dark Eyes,* Trad. (Scottish song) *Loch Lomond;* Wagner Tannhäuser, WWV70: *Evening Star*

Easy Clarinet Solos, vol. I - Student Level — MMO CD 3211

Harriet Wingreen, piano: Pieces for the beginning clarinetist. Suitable for first through third year of study.

Stephen Adams *The Holy City;* Beethoven *Für Elise;* di Capua *'O Sole Mio!;* Chiara *La Spagnola;* Chopin *Fantaisie Impromptu, op. 66 (theme);* Clay *I'll Sing Thee Songs of Araby,* Crouch *Kathleen Mavourneen;* Dacre *Daisy Bell (A Bicycle Built for Two);* d'Hardelot *Because;* Elgar *Pomp and Circumstance;* Fearis *Beautiful Isle of Somewhere;* Flotow Martha: *'Ah, So Pure' ('Ach, so Fromm');* Geibel *Kentucky Babe;* Grieg *Main Theme;* Harris *After the Ball;* Herbert *Serenade;* The Fortune Teller: *Gypsy Love Song;* Howe *Battle Hymn of the Republic;* Jacobs-Bond *I Love You Truly;* Jacobs-Bond (m); Stanton (l) *Just A-wearyin' for You;* Koven *O Promise Me;* Lehár Die Lustige Witwe (The Merry Widow): *'Vilja';* Lincke *The Glow Worm;* MacDowell *To a Wild Rose;* Meacham *American Patrol;* Nevin *Mighty Lak' a Rose; The Rosary;* Nugent *Sweet Rosie O'Grady;* Partichella *Mexican Hat Dance;* Rachmaninov *Piano Concerto No. 2 in C minor, op. 18 (Theme);* Rimsky-Korsakov *Song of India;* Rodrigues *La Cumparsita;* C. Sanders *Adios Muchachos;* Schubert *Who Is Sylvia?;* Sibelius *Finlandia;* Tchaikovsky *Marche Slave;* Trad. (American cowboy song) *Red River Valley;* Trad. (Hebrew melody) *Eili, Eili;* Trad. (Hebrew national anthem) *Hatikvoh (The Hope);* Trad. (Neapolitan song) *Santa Lucia;* Trotère *In Old Madrid;* Villoldo *El Choclo;* Ward, Charles E. *The Band Played On;* Ward, Samuel A. (m); Bates, Katharine Lee (l) *America, the Beautiful;* Yradier (Iradier) *La Paloma*

Easy Clarinet Solos, vol. II - Student Level — MMO CD 3212

Harriet Wingreen, piano: Volume Two is drawn from traditional and classical repertoire for clarinet and piano. Suitable for first-year through third-year students, this album will make practicing a true joy!

Jay Arnold *Blues in E-flat;* J.S. Bach *Jesu, Joy of Man's Desiring; Chorale No. 83;* Das Orgelbüchlein: *In Dulci Jubilo, BWV729 (chorale);* Bizet Carmen: *Toreador Song;* Borodin Prince Igor: *Melody (Moderato);* Brahms *Cradle Song;* Daniels *You Tell Me Your Dream;* Eastburn *Little Brown Jug;* Howard & Emerson *Hello! My Baby;* Lawlor The Sidewalks of New York: *The Sidewalks of New York;* Mendelssohn *Nocturne;* Offenbach *Bluebeard (scene);* Prokofiev *Peter and the Wolf, op. 67,* Rimsky-Korsakov *The Young Prince and the Young Princess; Sheherazade, op. 35;* Schubert *Valse Noble, op. 77, D969;* Smetana *The Moldau (theme);* Sousa *The High School Cadets; Manhattan Beach; The Rifle Regiment; The Stars & Stripes Forever;* J. Strauss, Jr. Der Zigeunerbaron (The Gypsy Baron): *Recruiting Song;* Josef Strauss *Fireproof Polka;* Stravinsky l'Oiseau de Feu (The Firebird): *Berceuse;* Sullivan H.M.S. Pinafore: *excerpt;* Thompson *Far Above Cayuga's Waters;* Trad. *I Ain't Gonna Study War No More; On Top of Old Smoky; Mr. Frog Went a'Courtin'!; When I Was Single; Old Paint; Careless Love; When the Saints Go Marching In;* Trad. (college song) *Spanish Guitar;* Trad. (English folk song) *Greensleeves;* Trad. (Folk song) *Black Is the Color of My True Love's Hair;* Trad. (Russian folk song) *The Cossack*

Take a Chorus B-flat/E-flat Instruments — MMO CD 7008

Ed Xiques, baritone, tenor, alto and soprano saxophone - Stan Getz, tenor sax; Hal McKusick, clarinet & flute; Jimmy Raney, guitar; George Duvivier, bass; Ed Shaughnessy, drums: Designed to give the student player valuable practice in the area of ensemble playing, as well as improvising. Also of interest to the professional, who can use it for enjoyment and practice. All ten arrangements have the instrumental parts included with example solos on each tune in smaller notes to serve as a guide.

Fools Rush In; I've Got It Bad and That Ain't Good; Just You, Just Me; How About You?; Sunday; Beta Minus; Jupiter; Spring Is Here; Darn that Dream; This Heart of Mine

Teacher's Partner *Basic Clarinet Studies for the Beginner* — MMO CD 3231

Scales in varied articulations, solos and duets with piano accompaniment. Covers first year of study and can be used with any method book. Addresses problems of pitch, rhythm, tone and articulation, presenting a professional model.

B-Flat Clarinet Tuning Instructions; G-major scale (using whole notes; then using quarter notes; then using half notes); F-major scale (using dotted half notes; then quarter notes; then using half notes followed by quarter notes); A-major scale (using half notes; then quarter note/quarter-rest alternations; then using eighth notes), B-flat major scale (using half, quarter and two eighth notes; then using a quarter followed by two eighths; then using a dotted quarter followed by an eighth); C-major scale (using whole notes; then sixteenth notes); D-major scale (using dotted whole notes; then quarter-sixteenth note combinations); Scale Cycle (6 scales); Solo in G major; Perky Piggies (duet in G major); Dream Waltz (solo in F major); Two in Three (duet in F major); March of the Toys (solo in A major); Graceful Partners (duet in A major); Romance (solo in B-flat major); Canon in B flat major; Banjo Song (solo in C major); Igorcentric (duet in C major), Peaceful Scene (duet in D major); Blueper (duet in B minor); Graduation Piece for B-flat clarinet

Twelve Classic Jazz Standards *B-flat/E-flat/Bass Clef Parts* — MMO CD 7010

Bryan Shaw, trumpet - The MMO All-Star Rhythm Section: These historic recordings of standards were made at Judson Hall in Manhattan in 1951 and feature, literally, legends in jazz. Beautiful renditions of some of the finest songs of the 20th century. These backgrounds feature accompaniments by such players as Nat Pierce and Don Abney (piano); Barry Galbraith and Jimmy Raney (guitar); Milt Hinton and Oscar Pettiford (bass); and Osie Johnson and Kenny Clarke (drums). Classic recordings! Includes sheet music for E-flat, B-flat and Bass Clef instruments. The pristine digital transfers of the original recordings put you right there with these jazz immortals! **(2CD Set)**

April in Paris; I Got Rhythm; Oh, Lady Be Good; Embraceable You; Porgy and Bess: *The Man I Love; Body and Soul; Poor Butterfly; Three Little Words; What Is This Thing Called Love?; Lover Come Back to Me; I Only Have Eyes for You, Sometimes I'm Happy*

Twelve More Classic Jazz Standards *B-flat/E-flat/Bass Clef Parts* — MMOCD7011

Tom Fischer, alto/tenor sax - The MMO All-Star Rhythm Section: This second album of historic recordings continues with a fabulous collection of standards. Your backgrounds for these classics are created by legends Don Abney (piano); Mundell Lowe and Jimmy Raney (guitar); Oscar Pettiford and Wilbur Ware (bass); and Kenny Clarke and Bobby Donaldson (drums). Includes sheet music for E-flat, B-flat and Bass Clef instruments. A true time machine to the greatest days of jazz accompaniments, in digitally remastered sound. **(2CD Set)**

You Go to My Head; Strike Up the Band; I Cover the Waterfront; Too Marvelous for Words; Crazy Rhythm; Don't Take Your Love From Me; Just One of Those Things; My Heart Stood Still; I May Be Wrong (But I Think You're Wonderful) [from the 1929 revue]; When Your Lover Has Gone; Fine and Dandy; Jeepers Creepers

World Favorites *Student Editions, 41 Easy Selections (1st-3rd year)* — MMO CD 3244

Harriet Wingreen, piano: The New York Philharmonic's legendary pianist, Harriet Wingreen, accompanies you in forty-one selections from around the world, chosen for their beauty and ease of performance. Certain to delight the beginning student.

Balfe *Then You'll Remember Me;* Becucci *Tesoro Mio;* di Capua *'O Sole Mio!;* Chopin *Etude, op. 10, no. 3;* Daly *Chicken Reel;* Debussy *Clair de Lune;* d'Hardelot *Because;* Dresser *On the Banks of the Wabash;* Evans *In the Good Old Summertime;* Franck Messe solennelle, op. 12, M61: *5. Panis Angelicus (O Lord Most Holy);* Gruber *Silent Night;* Herbert *Romany Life;* J.H. Hopkins *We Three Kings of Orient Are;* Jessel *Parade of the Tin Soldiers;* Kennedy *Star of the East;* Lehár Die Lustige Witwe (The Merry Widow): *The Merry Widow Waltz;* Lincke *The Glow Worm;* MacDowell *To a Wild Rose; To a Water Lily;* Marchetti *Fascination;* L. Mason *Nearer, My God, to Thee;* Mendelssohn *Hark, the Herald Angels Sing;* Murray *Away in a Manger/Silent Night;* Neidlinger, W.H. *The Birthday of a King;* Nevin *Mighty Lak' a Rose;* Olcott *My Wild Irish Rose;* Poulton *Aura Lee;* Reading *Come All Ye Faithful;* Spilman *Flow Gently, Sweet Afton;* Trad. *He's Got the Whole World in His Hands;* Trad. (American cowboy song) *The Yellow Rose of Texas; Red River Valley;* Trad. (English folk song) *Greensleeves;* Trad. (Folk song) *Black Is the Color of My True Love's Hair;* Trad. (Irish melody) *Londonderry Air;* Trad. (Irish song) *Sweet Molly Malone;* Trad. (Scottish song) *Blue Bells of Scotland;* Trad. (Spiritual) *Deep River;* Trad. (U.S. Army Song) *Caisson Song;* Trad. (U.S. Marine Corps Song) *The Marines' Hymn;* Trad. (Welsh song) *All through the Night;* Yradier (Iradier) *La Paloma*

For our full catalogue of clarinet releases, including more popular and jazz titles, classical concerti, chamber works and master classes visit us on the web at

www.musicminusone.com

Call 1-800 669-7464 in the USA • 914 592-1188 International • Fax: 914 592-2751
email: mmogroup@musicminusone.com

MUSIC MINUS ONE
50 Executive Boulevard
Elmsford, New York 10523-1325
800-669-7464 (U.S.)/914-592-1188 (International)

www.musicminusone.com
e-mail: mmogroup@musicminusone.com